Abused to Blessed

ABUSED

TO

BLESSED

Breaking My Silence
on How God Healed
My Life

By Kathy Jennings

XULON PRESS

Xulon Press
2301 Lucien Way #415
Maitland, FL 32751
407.339.4217
www.xulonpress.com

Unless otherwise indicated, Scripture quotations taken from the King
James Version (KJV)–*public domain.*

Printed in the United States of America.

ISBN-13: 978-1-5456-7957-9

DEDICATION

I dedicate this book to my awesome God who has loved me, supported me, and strengthened me through whatever I have and will go through, and whatever I do. He has taught me I am already healed, made whole, and am more than a conqueror. He has healed my life, taught me the God-kind of faith, and what being loved and normal is all about.

I also want to acknowledge my husband who helped me write and re-write every page, and who has been by my side and supported me through my trials for over thirty-three years. Without him, taking me out of that bad environment, protecting me from my family's drama, encouraging me, and helping every step along the way, this book, my healing, my growth, and my victories with God would not have been possible.

Also, thank you to my daughter and son, Laura and Tony, for loving mom even through the bad times.

TABLE OF CONTENTS

ABUSED TO BLESSED

Y ou may wonder why on earth I wrote this book? The answer is simple. Because God told me to. In this crazy, mixed up, complicated world, He simply told me to simply write a simple book.

He told me to write it so people could learn, from reading my story, how they can heal from their wounds. God's truth can heal you, both inside emotionally and outside, concerning everything in your life. God's wholeness will heal your life, and His anointing will put you back together, brick by brick, layer by layer, month by month, year by year.

This book is about sexual abuse, trauma, and violation. I want to show you there is a devil and he is real. This book is about being led astray, making mistakes, and falling into the pit of darkness Satan always prepares for us to keep us from our destiny. You will see how he tried numerous times to put me out of commission and kill me on the spot.

God inspired me, and told me to tell the truth of what happened to me, so His people would be healed and know His truth, which is you are already healed in Jesus' name. My story particularly will help people who have been abused, suffered trauma, were attacked and shattered, and who feel broken. He WILL help you.

I was rescued and saved for a greater purpose. I was healed from head to toe, emotionally, physically, mentally, and spiritually, to achieve a balance of wholeness only the Creator is capable of giving. God will show you the way through His Word that any situation can be changed and healed if you believe him.

I have never told my story. It's a bit wild and "out there". Many people don't believe in the stuff I'm going to share. I don't care. It happened, just how I explain. Keep an open mind; you never know, you might just get something out of my experiences.)

First, I'll share a part of my life to illustrate what happened; where I was and what went down. I will explain the horrible things that hurt me when I was a child, a teen, a married woman, and a mother. Then you will learn about how, in all my pain, I was picked up out of the trap Satan set for me and gradually became saved, healed, and anointed. You will learn practical information on how I dealt with my problems, step by step, and how I triumphed over the deceiver, stepping on his scrawny neck. Many of the things I've learned are from today's most powerful Christian ministries, from years of studying, and from many friends and family.

Let's take a walk now down the path together so you too can learn how to be healed from abuse in your life and become blessed wherever you walk.

Thank you, Jesus!

Chapter 1

A DYSFUNCTIONAL FAMILY

The Bible is clear that any form of abuse is unacceptable. God hates the idea of anyone being abused. The Bible lays out how we are to treat those we love. It instructs us to share sacrificial love—love that yearns for the absolute very best for every person. The Bible does not specifically use the term "child abuse." It does tell us children have a special place in God's heart, and anyone who harms a child is inviting God's wrath upon himself.

I came from a broken home. There was a lot of screaming and yelling. There was a lot of physical and mental fighting; not much peace to say the least. Fear was always in the air, every day, because I never knew if someone was going to blow up at me or leave me alone. I was on edge all the time. My home life was anything but normal. It was definitely dysfunctional.

I was abused emotionally, mentally, and physically, between the ages of eight to twenty-one. My mother's drama was yelling and screaming, then she used to beat the crap out of me for the littlest thing. I was beaten and molested by family members—people who were supposed to love me and protect me.

Later in years, I would understand a generational curse plagued my family and was delivered unto me. There was a door opened in my family tree which led to the abuse I suffered.

At this point, I need to define a few things. What is a curse? In his book, *Unmasking the Devil,* John Ramirez explains a curse is a judgment from God against a person or persons for disobeying His word, or to state it differently, committing sin. Under a curse, doors are opened in your life for demons to enter and begin their work of disrupting your world. These demons can bring disease, torment, strife, destruction, and death. [1]

Once a door is opened, a generational curse can remain upon your family tree. It perpetuates itself in your family and down the line of your relatives. This curse can go three or four generations or can go back ten generations. Now, some would say this is Old Testament thinking, but there is evidence from many sources, and from my own life, that suggest generational curses are real and do effect believers and non-believers if not dealt with.

A little more background data. When I refer to "The Curse" it means the original Earth curse that Adam got us into. I place the scripture reference here.

"Then to Adam the LORD God said, "Because you
have listened [attentively] to the voice of your wife,
and have eaten [fruit] from the tree about which I
commanded you, saying, 'You shall not eat of it';
The ground is [now] under a curse because of you;
In sorrow *and* toil you shall eat [the fruit] of it
All the days of your life.
Both thorns and thistles it shall grow for you;
And you shall eat the plants of the field.
By the sweat of your face
You will eat bread
Until you return to the ground,
For from it you were taken;
For you are dust,
And to dust you shall return." (Genesis 3:17-19 AMP)

The Jezebel Spirit was operating in my life and my family's. Let me explain here, also. Jezebel was a real person in the Bible, the wife of King Ahab, the King of Israel. She was an evil women who tried to murder all of God's prophets. How does this translate to present day? We call the spirit of Jezebel, who is alive and well, a demonic murderous spirit who operates on our fears, deals in witchcraft, fosters sexual abuse, causes strife, destroys churches, and causes division between people and families. All this I learned while God was healing me during my study times. [2]

The curse from the Jezebel spirit was destroying my parents' marriage and separating our family. It kept my parents fighting and yelling at each other, and then they would take it out on me and my sisters. We couldn't live together as a family because my parents could not get along. The spirit of division had separated us.

What I learned in hindsight was, when you have something important to do for the Lord, Satan will try to come to take you out. He keeps putting people in your path to abuse you, then makes it look like it's your own fault when, in reality, you have done nothing wrong to bring this on. John 10:10 says Satan comes to steal, kill, and destroy, but Jesus came that you may have life and have it more abundantly.

Satan set out to destroy me and those I care for.

I wanted to be loved, but was rejected and abused. We were living on Fifth Street at the time. It was obvious my parents could not get along, so one night they sat all three of us girls down on the couch and said they were getting a divorce. My mother asked us who we wanted to live with, then my Dad asked us. Then they fought over who was going to get custody over us. They pitted each sibling against the other, and caused a horrible wound in all of us. How can a child pick one parent over the other?

Right after the custody battle, my mother took off. She must have gone to live with her boyfriend. My Dad was a buffer at a shop and he was never home; he was either working or carousing.

I was literally abandoned by both parents. I was left by myself with two sisters, and we basically took care of ourselves. I went to kindergarten in the afternoon. My sisters came home from school for lunch and walked me to school and back every day. I was basically left alone all morning by myself. I really know what alone feels like. What a thing to go through when you're six or seven years old.

There was never enough food in the house. All I can remember is a bare refrigerator and cupboards, and how empty the house felt. I remember my sisters cooking grilled cheese sandwiches, and tomato soup sometimes. I remember tuna fish sandwiches and eggs sometimes. Once in a while there were hot dogs and hamburgers, but it was few and far between.

I learned years later that my mom moved out because my dad beat her up a lot. That did not make things any better in my mind. I knew, however, my parents loved us the best they knew how. They did show it at times, tried to hug us and make up for the bad things, but there was so much anger in that house that it overshadowed any love that was present.

My dad I really dearly loved. I only lived with him a short time in our Fifth St. home. My siblings and I had a lot of fun with him on his boat. Vacations, movies, and dinner were his big things. He would stop at the corner store on the way to the lake and get candy for me to enjoy on the boat. When I was a teen, he moved to St. Louis to live with his sister.

After I graduated from high school, my dad died. I have good and bad memories of him. He loved me, but the fighting in the house of Fifth St. was terrible and took its toll. There were some good times in our home though My mom loved to cook dinner for her family. Mom would take us to church and to bible study class when we were little. We all went on vacation together. I can't say we didn't have some fun or that we didn't all love each other, but you always knew the drama would come back.

We moved out to a more rural setting and into a condemned house. This was when I was in second grade. The divorce between my mom and dad was almost final when we had to move out of the Fifth Street house. A few months later the divorce was final. Mom married her boyfriend on Memorial Day weekend later that year.

My mom, my new step-dad, and my sisters and I had to work all the time on the condemned house to bring it up to code and make it livable. I remember pulling up in the driveway for the first time and seeing the big condemned sign tacked to the side of the house. The place was a mess. There was mismatched carpet everywhere, the insides were dirty and buggy, and there was no running water. It also badly needed paint The house didn't have a hot water tank and the septic system was backed up and needed to be replaced. It smelled like a sewer. I'll never forget that smell.

Chapter 2

THE ABUSE

The generational curse, the one that steals from, kills, and destroys your life, was running rampant in my life and my family's. My step-dad was an alcoholic with issues about women, and he molested me several times between the ages of eight and twenty-one. He would always talk sexually to me and made sexual advances as well. He talked dirty all the time, and made me and others feel devalued all the time. (No young girl should be talked to the way he talked to me. Nobody should be talked to that way.) One day I came home from work when I was about nineteen or twenty years old. There was a clean pile of laundry laying on my bed. On top of the pile was my underwear with a raw hot dog laying inside. He had put it there because he had a twisted mind. It was sick. I was also molested by another man close to the family.

The same kind of fighting and abuse continued in the new house just as much as it did in the old house. My mom and step-dad drank a lot and fought a lot; it was almost constant. One time they came home from the bar, drinking and fighting, and throwing dishes. My step-dad pulled out a gun on my mom and she laid on the couch all night with a gun to her head. Finally, he told her he was going to kill her, but it wasn't going to be that night. I saw the whole thing and heard every word, then I went and hid in my room. I cried all night long.

But Satan was the one really behind this constantly happening abuse. I used to go to bed as a young girl crying myself to sleep and asking God to please take me away from this home, away from the abuse of my mom and step-dad.

At the age of twenty-one, I moved out of my mom and step-dad's house. I lived on my own until I was twenty-four years old. I met my husband, Mike, when I was twenty-four. He would come into the convenience store where I worked every morning and buy coffee and donuts. I made great coffee and donuts. I guess that's what got his attention.

I know God sent Mike to save me from the abuse I suffered as a child, and he did. However, I don't think he knew what he was getting himself into. He wasn't used to my mother's drama and yelling. She would scream at us and chase us around in the car. She would stalk us sometimes all day so she could get her claws in us. He had never seen people act this way before. He was definitely not used to how my family acted with each other.

I married Mike when I was twenty-five. At twenty-eight, I had our daughter, and, at thirty-four, I had our son. All along, Satan would put people in my path to keep some kind of turmoil or rejection going. My mother was not nice at all to us after we got married and had a family. Her crazy, mostly verbal abuse would not stop no matter what Mike and I did.

Eventually, I walked away from my family for nine years. My mom, step-dad, sisters, cousins—everybody. I was angry, rejected, abused, hurt, and in pain at the time. We could not let any of them talk to us or our kids or else the verbal abuse would start all over again. That's when I finally got some peace.

I guess my mom didn't know how to handle my new life. She herself was very beaten down from both husbands, physically and mentally. By this time, she was almost in her 60's and she still did not know what to do. My mother had her way of seeing life. It wasn't always the right way, and it didn't always work for her either.

When I walked away from my parents, I told my husband about it all—the physical, sexual, and mental abuse; being beaten, violated, and tormented; the never ending pain of being devalued; how I did not feel protected by my parents from the molestation I did not feel protected from my parents or step-dad. Mike told me he would do anything he had to in order to protect me.

I told my mom I had told my husband about it all, and she was so mad at me because now somebody else knew the family's dark secret. She wrote me a nasty letter saying I did not have any right to tell my husband. Yet, what do you do when you are violated and molested by your step-dad and other men and your mother doesn't do anything about it? Mom did not believe me. Nobody, that is outside family and friends, really knew what I experienced growing up. They did not have a clue what I went through and what Mike and I went through as a couple.

So even as sad as I was as a child, when I grew to adulthood, I began to see life differently. Thank God He changed my life. He really understood what happened. I always knew as a kid God loved me, but as I grow older, I am now realizing just how much! God and His Bible have taught me so much.

I am so sad my parents did not understand the curse haunting us—that it was alive and well in their lives, and that we all were living it. My heart loves them so much and I truly forgive them. I know they loved me the best they knew how. They were just in so much pain themselves. I am so grateful and blessed God showed me and told me the truth, healing me from all of it. I love you Mom and Dad, Thank you for giving me life, because my God is awesome for giving me my life back.

Today I miss them all, and if I had the chance to change our past, I would. I found out you never know how much you love someone until they are not with you. I so wish someone would have showed me about this curse thing when I was younger.

If you have a parent who is not capable of showing up and not capable of reflecting you back through eyes of love, know it will have a big impact upon your sense of self-worth. A child always thinks it's his or her fault because he or she cannot blame the adult because the child depends on them for survival. It takes a long time to get over this falsely assumed guilt. I have come to realize it wasn't that I was not loveable, because I was. It was because my parents had issues. When I became aware of that, I was able to have tremendous empathy for them and finally forgive them.

People don't understand generational curses or want to talk about them either, but they are real. I don't think my parents knew anything about them. They didn't know the truth in His Word, so they did the best they could with what they knew.

I want to say I'm sorry to my family because, after I went through all of this nightmare and hell, I distanced myself from all my family and friends. My husband and I really did not want any more drama in our lives. I also was ashamed for my family and for me. But as it turned out, they did not want to talk to me either.

I decided to love my family anyway, something I learned from reading Joyce Myers. I also learned that Satan wanted me to feel shame and hide so I would not be able to do my assignment from God. The best part is, through it all, God's the one who helped me overcome it.

Ten years went by. Mike and I were still trying to figure things out in our life. We were trying to find a way to fill up our lives. Mike suffered from depression over the years and that led to our looking for some relief. What happened next was a mind-boggling nightmare.

Chapter 3

THE CHURCH

I was incredibly naive to what was about to happen to me next. A friend of the family told me about this metaphysical-spiritualist church in my town. What I did not know was Satan was behind this set up, and he was leading us into something we did not understand.

So Mike went to check it out alone to see what it was all about. He was given a message from a "spirit" and a strange thing happened to him. ["Spirit" is a term used in the spiritualist church that refers to all spiritual entities who come through and give messages to the living. The term does not mean the Holy Spirit, and it does not mean your spirit. By all accounts and observations, it is very likely a demonic spirit.]. When he was sitting in the pew one evening, he felt something tap him on the shoulder from behind. When he turned to look back, nobody was there. Nobody was sitting behind him. From what I know now, that's when a demon followed him home and began messing with our life.

Mike went back for more services to figure out what was going on, because neither of us had ever seen anything like these services before. It was like a normal church service, but with personal healing, and everyone got a message from the "spirit" channeled by the pastor or an assistant from the platform each time. It was new, it was shocking, and it was enthralling all at the same time.

However, Mike was probably being led by the demon. He received more messages and healings What we didn't know was Satan was working his wiles among us all.

Mike and I thought it was ok and our kids stayed with Grandma and Grampa while we went to services on Sunday evenings. I do admit I was confused about it all and very naive to all this new information. This church was way different than anything else we had ever seen. I had been raised Protestant. Mike and I were married in a Methodist church and we somehow just stopped going. Little did we know we were walking into Satan's trap to mire us in this church, and that he was working behind the scenes to keep us out of the will of God.

A few times I ran in to the lady minister from the church at the grocery store. It seemed like a coincidence, but now I wonder if it was a part of Satan's ploy. This woman and I would chat, and we gradually became friends. The lady minister, if that's what you want to call her, eventually gave me a personal reading after hours. (Later on I would find out she was a medium. I had no idea. I didn't even know what a medium was.) One session turned into two and then more. Later, I found out how this changed my life for the worse.

There was one particular event that kept me going back for more readings. It happened on a Sunday morning in early summer. I was sleeping on the couch and I heard a voice say to me "Kathy." I woke up, and across the room I saw my Dad sitting in a chair! It startled me because he had been dead since 1979., It was now 1996.

I need to relate what I now know about this kind of appearance. Please note in reality it was not my Dad. Many, many times, the devil and his demons pose as our loved ones to throw us off and lead us down a path of destruction. They even have the ability to mimic your loved one's voice to the tee. I have no doubt that this was the case here.

I had to know more. I had so many questions for my Dad because he died so young. I did not get to see him for years after he left and went to Missouri to live with his sister, my aunt, but I did get to see him about a week before he died. So many lies had been told in my family. I really wanted to get at some of the truth.

I thought I was getting emotional healing with each session, but really the demon was trying to get its hooks in me, to befriend me, all to lure me in and then turn on me (later on I would identify it as the Jezebel Spirit). I even went to some psychic fairs, had palm readings, etc., in search of more answers. I didn't know it at the time but it was all lies, lies, lies!

Much later I read John Ramirez's book *Out of the Devil's Cauldron*. In it he says mediums are those who lend their bodies to demonic spirits to speak and perform their works. These demons are murderers, and they are assigned to destroy you and kill you. I did not know my sessions with mediums and psychics would open up the satanic world to come at me.[3]

The lady minister also had group meditation sessions. She would gather a circle of people together and try to get them to open up so a spirit could enter their bodies and speak through them. I did not personally see this, but my husband saw it happen. She was also trying to ordain people to be like her, the devil on the platform. Essentially, she was recruiting people to be satanic ministers. [This was something else my husband and I learned after reading John Ramirez's book.][4]

Chapter 1

THE LIE

The lady minister preached we have spirit guides and told us they tell us what to do in our lives. Know right now there are no such thing as spirit guides. This is a lie from hell. All these so called "spirit guides" want to do is kill, steal, and destroy your life. They are evil spirits sent by Satan. Don't believe anyone who tells you the spirit guide lie. Although that person will say it is all good, these beings bring no love; it's all hate. These demons are against you; they hate you. It may not seem like it in the beginning, as they appear kind and all knowing, and act like they want to help you, but, sooner or later, they become darker and eviler until they have you in the grip of their control.

This demonic force will go after you. They will look to bring you into the church and make you think the messages you're getting come directly from God. This is their wickedness and how they lead innocent people to stray from God's love. There is no truth in them or what they say. They will try to break your body down to sickness and disease as well as steal your money or make you lose your financial support. Nothing pleases these evil beings more than seeing you living in poverty with no hope. And they will make you think there is no hope at all for you; that you are far beyond worth of rescuing and that you are trapped forever in a dark, dark pit from hell with no way out. These are all dirty lies.

You may think it's ok to participate in psychic readings but strange things will happen to you because you are opening the door to Satan without realizing what will happen to you. Psychic readings may become your norm as well as tarot cards and other forms of divination. All this is designed to stroke your ego and make you believe you can become psychic or have some sort of power over others.

Strange things happened to me. My bed at times shook and vibrated without cause. I would be lying in bed and my body suddenly would be totally paralyzed and frozen; I could not move. I also saw dark shadows in my home.

Such things come about because you opened the door for Satan to attack you. He will lead you away from the Lord and cut you off from God because you've put another god before Him and He can't help you then. Satan will start telling you what to say and do. He will give you a suggestion, like I see a new job in your life, I see you getting sick, you need to watch out for this and that, I see you getting a divorce, someone wants to hurt you, or you will receive this or that.

If you agree with what he says, then he will make it happen because you have given him the authority to interfere in your life. He'll make you think you are getting messages from your loved ones in heaven. Not true! He'll go after your money and your health. Your possessions will break down, such as your car; you'll have car accidents. Things will happen in your family to promote unforgiveness. Satan will divide your family; you won't want to talk to them. He'll try to keep you in offense and strife to keep your family all churned up. The devil and his demonic forces will come after you. They will make you go in all kinds of directions.

The evil forces will make you believe they are the authority in your life. The truth is you are spiritually cut off from God and they can therefore take authority over YOU. The truth is that we have authority over them; it's not the other way around. The only thing these demons bring is strife, hate, and unforgiveness. They will put you in situations that are difficult and abusive, and make you think you deserve such treatment. They will try to destroy generations of family, and they will turn you against anyone who resists. They are deceitful. They try to destroy marriages by encouraging people to have affairs. Make no covenant with them for they are the devil.

Remember, when you get a reading from a psychic, Satan will always make suggestions to use you. You will hear out of the mouth of the medium, "I see a divorce, I see sickness, I see you leaving a job, I see money coming, or worse leaving". These are *all lies*. Satan goes to work making these lies happen in your life. You are not connected to God when he plays with you like this. You are in danger. All the cards from a tarot deck are bad news. People think tarot is only cool entertainment, but it is not. The cards are an instrument of destruction and another way for Satan to get into your life as you are giving him permission to screw with you on a new level.

I asked for help. Not one person in that church wanted to help me. She was just coming after me, attacking me. Yes, I did forgive her and asked God to help her. I prayed for her, asked God to take her out of my life. He did, but I was still dealing with the trauma from her demonic forces.

I went through hell for years. Evil is real and it happens. Jezebel and her demonic forces know that the judgement is near and the curse is on her, and that she has to pay seven times seven back to me because they tried to kill me not once, but several times. Whatever you do, please walk in the Kingdom of God, not the Kingdom of Darkness.

Meanwhile, Jezebel's spirit was behind it all, and we did not know it. Anytime you ever try to do something like this, know the enemy is already behind it. We were both young and stupid, so naive, and now have so much regret.

Chapter 5

THE VIOLENT ATTACKS

October 31, 1999 was when all hell broke loose. It started out with me being the chairperson of the service that night. That means, basically, you're the ringmaster for the circus. You introduce everybody, you read out loud, and you help with the offering. I was put on the spot that night. The lady minister begged me to run the service as there was nobody else who could do it. I was petrified,

I was on the platform with her on Halloween night. I did a good job running the service but I was drained from it; I must have been weak. But I had conquered my fear of public speaking. It was late when I went home, half in a daze, and went to bed. I really needed some rest that night. However, I could not sleep.

I was lying in bed when I soon became aware of intense pressure on my body as if a huge weight had been placed upon me. I could not move, I could not scream. It felt like I was being beaten with a rod. My arms, legs, and body were under attack by something. It almost felt like bullets pounding my body.

At the same time, I could hear literally in my ear loud screaming and noise that was horrifying. I could also hear obscenities and verbal attacks directed right at me. I got cold and hot, and it fluctuated all over my body on and off. I was terrified, crying and screaming when I could.

I woke the whole house up, asking my husband and kids to help me. They were dumbfounded and scared. We were up all night and I did not sleep at all. I was under attack by Satan and his demons. He was trying to break down my body, tormenting me with loud drama, yelling, and screaming, beating my body down trying to kill me that night. It went on for a long time. I told whatever was coming at me to stop, but it would not stop.

I did not understand what was happening to me. The attacks continued day and night. This thing had a plan to keep me sleep deprived to wear my body out and kill me. It kept coming at me and coming at me. It did not slow down or give up easily.

We went back into the church several times to see if we could find some answers as to why all this was happening to me. The lady minister wanted me to believe I had to live with this terrible condition, there was no way out, and the situation could not change. She said I had to live with this affliction and the violent attacks, and it would never get better. She said I should just give up and learn to get along with whatever was tormenting me. I even told her to stop what she was doing and take this off of me, and she would not.

We stopped going to that evil church after that. However, she would call me at all hours, and kept coming over my house uninvited, begging us to come back. I think she just wanted to see how far the affliction had progressed and admire her handy work. She even went as far as to say the spirit [really a demon] wanted to kill me! Through it all, she knew Satan had put a hit on me. I know she was behind this affliction because she admitted it in private days before when nobody else was around to hear. She was not remorseful at all, though, because she believed it had nothing to do with her. I think that is what hurt me most of all.

I did a lot of crying during this period of attack, and I stayed inside away from people. Talking about it was terrible. That is what Satan's plan was and what he wanted. It was hard to cope with. I had never been exposed to stuff like this before, let alone left by myself to understand what was happening to me.

I coped with the spiritual attack and the generational curse by surrounding myself with the strength and healing power of God's word. I leave you with some of my favorite scriptures.

"Finally, my brethren, be strong in the Lord, and in the power of his might. Put on the whole armour of God, that ye may be able to stand against the wiles of the devil. For we wrestle not against flesh and blood, but against principalities, against powers, against the rulers of the darkness of this world, against spiritual wickedness in high places. Wherefore take unto you the whole armour of God, that ye may be able to withstand in the evil day, and having done all, to stand. Stand therefore, having your loins girt about with truth, and having on the breastplate of righteousness; And your feet shod with the preparation of the gospel of peace; Above all, taking the shield of faith, wherewith ye shall be able to quench all the fiery darts of the wicked. And take the helmet of salvation, and the sword of the Spirit, which is the word of God." (Ephesians 6:10-17 KJV)

"Verily I say unto you, whatsoever ye shall bind on earth shall be bound in heaven: and whatsoever ye shall loose on earth shall be loosed in heaven. Again I say unto you, that if two of you shall agree on earth as touching anything that they shall ask, it shall be done for them of my Father which is in heaven. For where two or three are gathered together in my name, there am I in the midst of them." (Matthew 18:18-20 KJV)

"Behold, I give unto you power to tread on serpents and scorpions, and over all the power of the enemy: and nothing shall by any means hurt you." (Luke 10:19 KJV).

"And God said, Let us make man in our image, after our likeness: and let them have dominion over the fish of the sea, and over the fowl of the air, and over the cattle, and over all the earth, and over every creeping thing that creepeth upon the earth. So God created man in his own image, in the image of God created he him; male and female created he them. And God blessed them, and God said unto them, Be fruitful, and multiply, and replenish the earth, and subdue it: and have dominion over the fish of the sea, and over the fowl of the air, and over every living thing that moveth upon the earth." (Genesis 1:26-28 KJV)

Chapter 6

THE DEVIL IN DISGUISE

S atan went to work among us making bad things happen in our lives. This was after my husband and I left the church and were away for some time. The demons came at us with destruction, poverty, attacks, sickness, and more.

We started hearing things from former members. I'm not the only one who was attacked; there were others. We heard terrible things had happened to people. People lost jobs, income, even their health, and sometimes they felt they could not get out of bed each day. Some members of that evil church even died. They did not even know why these things happened. Later people would understand the lady minister was behind it all with the Devil as her partner.

It was always her and her devils. Some members were told never to come back to the church because they had found out things the lady minister had been doing that she did not want anyone to know. We know of several people who were attacked by her demons. They all got sick for a long time with different ailments and eventually were unable to work and lost their jobs. One of them even lost their apartment and had to move. They were out of work for a year or longer before they were able to get back on track.

The lady minister never told people she was sorry, and she never took responsibility for her actions. She always acted like she had never done anything wrong. She told lies through the spirit guides that came and went from her body. The messages that came through her sounded like they were given from a loved one who had passed, and you would hear it through her voice. They would say things like, "It's time for you to pull up stakes and find another job, where you are right now does not serve you anymore." Or things like "You need to get in this person's face because they are doing you a disservice behind your back," or something to the effect that you needed to take classes, do exercises, or practice mediation to open up and further advance. They would say a guide wanted to work with you on healing, or on raising your kids, or any number of seemingly random things that did not sound like it was relevant to you. Then, on the other side, you could get a message directly from a loved one regarding something nobody knew about, only you.

The lady minister would stand on the platform and at times you could see a shadow or a piece of an aura standing beside her. When a message was given, you could see the faint figure assume the shape of her body and speak through her voice. She would say things like, "If you follow me you will be just like God." She would teach that we had seven spirit guides who followed us our whole life. They wanted to help us, they loved us, and would always be around to help us evolve. They were all knowing, and the more they helped us, the faster and higher they would evolve along with us.

What most of the church's members didn't know was the lady minister was ordaining as many followers/ministers as she could, grooming them to be just like her, encouraging all who would do the exercises with her to open themselves up to give messages the same way she did. She also had all the church's bibles, hymnals, and reference books changed so references to certain things, like the blood of Jesus, were removed. She also would have no part of communion especially with red wine. It had to be white wine. Nobody thought anything of it at the time, but, looking back on it from today, these were major red flags signaling something was seriously wrong.

From where I stand today, and from years of Bible study, I really think she was possessed by Satan and their joint goal was to possess all of us. I really do not think the church members knew any of this.

This woman and Satan had evil toward me. She had many demons inside of her. She told us she was very angry we left the church. She channeled evil spirits to attack me. She was trying to get the spirit guides (really devils) to enter my body and possess me. She was trying to kill me. One time, she told me if things were THAT bad I should kill myself so I could come back in another life and start over.

I had to break the evil force away from us. Thank you, God, for saving my life.

Chapter 7

THE FIGHT BACK

After I walked away from her church, I found out the truth from God. I was praying with a friend and he recommended I get an exorcism as the voices and the torment were still occurring. I did not join another church for a while. I went to see a lot of different people for help. During this time, I fervently studied the Bible. I went to a Bible-based church where they were filled with the Holy Spirit and prayed in tongues.

At this time, Mike and I were trying to sell our mobile home to move on with our life. It had been on the market for a long, long time. I knew it was stuck because of the affliction I had. I appealed to the pastor for help. I went to the bible study class on Wednesday nights for about a month. One night, fifteen people gathered around me, put their hands on me, and started praying. I felt so different. I had never felt love like that. Something broke, I felt better, and the next day our mobile home sold.

Next, my dear friend in Florida told me I needed to call Loraine Warren in Connecticut. She was a famous demonologist who, with her husband, wrote books and fought the devil for many years. I contacted her and had several conversations. We became friends, and she recommended several Catholic priests I needed to visit. One was fairly close by, about 75 miles from the house. The other one was in Connecticut. I spent time with both of them. I went to Catechism class and I learned a lot.

I had two exorcisms in Connecticut about a month a part. We went to Connecticut for the exorcisms because there was nobody in Michigan who could help us. We drove all the way to Stamford, Connecticut where we met the priest and a demonologist who was an ex-policeman. He did security for the priest; he was to be in the same room and he did carry a gun to protect the priest.

We were very nervous and uneasy. We were at a private office somewhere in Connecticut. They explained everything that would happen during the rite. We talked, trying to get to know each other and the demonologist. We all prayed, including saying the Lord's Prayer. The priest sprinkled holy water and read the rite out loud to my face, looking into my eyes. I felt strange and anxious. After he was done, though, I did feel better, lighter. He said I was in pretty good control of the entity because he did not see a huge reaction from me or anything else during the prayers. He advised us to come back in about a month, and so we did.

The same thing happened the second time, except there were four more people in the room; a couple of paranormal investigators and two demonologists. After the rite, the priest said he could tell the demon was greatly weakened. I was, as a matter of fact, feeling much better. They had me go down to the corner store and buy five gallons of spring water which the priest blessed, turning it into holy water. We took five gallons back with us to Michigan where I did use it for a while afterwards when I had bad days. The demon was weakened, I could tell there was no doubt about it. Information from the priests, Lorraine Warren, and the demonologists indicated they could tell the demon that was bothering me was around me, not in me, and he was very much weakened.

I joined the Catholic church and made the commute to the nearest church for about a year, but it just got too expensive to drive seventy-five miles each week to do so. I was broke. So, the

Catholic church basically told me to keep up my prayers, go get a job, and get on with my life. One thing I'd like to share about the Catholic church is that they do not like to acknowledge that more and more people are having problems with demonic forces. They know that it is a huge problem and it's getting worse by the year, yet there are no procedures or policies in place to help people who ask for it. There definitely isn't any help that we know of in Michigan. None of the Catholic churches we called in our area would even talk to us about it.

After Mike and I went home, a couple of months later, I got a job and we started looking for a house. That was about the end of 2004. We couldn't find a house we could live in because all of the ones we looked at had had cats living in them and Mike is allergic to cats. So we decided to build our house. Half way through the building, though, Mike lost his job. We struggled a lot but managed to finish the house and moved in February 2007. Then, Mike had to go look for a new job. We struggled every day of the week trying to make ends meet. It was not the easiest times in our life. Mike finally found a job with help from friends and family, so we were able keep the house.

A while went by, some months maybe, but I don't exactly remember. One day, I was surfing through the channels of Christian TV and I came across Kenneth Copeland Ministries. He changed my life forever. He taught me how to have faith in God's Word. He and his wife, Gloria, from their teachings, taught me how to have faith in God's healing. They taught me how to have authority over Satan in Jesus' name; authority over poverty and fear. They taught me how to speak the anointing over my life. They taught me how to prosper in troubled times.

Let me tell you, when I finally learned about my authority over fear, that's when I knew Satan and all of his demons were finished. In Jesus' name. That's when I knew all these things that happened to me were from Satan and her. I declared he could not put anything on me anymore, and the torment stopped. I was free!

Do not put another god before Him. False gods are all of the devil. There is only one God and the only way to Him is through Jesus. Only pray to the Father in Jesus' name.

When you know the authority you have through Jesus, the devil is powerless over you. Reach out to the Lord like it says in Psalm 35.

> "Draw out also the spear, and stop the way against them that persecute me: say unto my soul, I am thy salvation. Let them be confounded and put to shame that seek after my soul: let them be turned back and brought to confusion that devise my hurt. Let them be as chaff before the wind: and let the angel of the Lord chase them. Let their way be dark and slippery: and let the angel of the Lord persecute them." (Psalm 35:3-6 KJV)

It makes me angry seeing the abuse happening all over the world and how God gets blamed for it. It is actually the god of this world, Satan, abusing and victimizing people. He uses fear and torment to attack you, and he likes to use it over and over again. Satan uses other people to abuse you too, and fills them with the belief they have power over you. Stand up, take your authority back, and tell the truth when you're going through abuse, trauma, rape and sexual abuse, etc. Satan's goal is to make you feel powerless, devalued, and broken. He wants to make you feel that you deserve such horrible treatment. How does any young girl of any age (or boy for that matter) deserve this? Do not let Satan torment you with his lies! God will help you with your problems and give you His assistance.

Jesus gave His life so that we may have life. Jesus is the Healer; He healed them all. There is an enemy named Satan who prowls around seeking to steal your blessing. Use the strength of the Lord to fight him off.

"Surely he hath borne our griefs, and carried our sorrows: yet we did esteem him stricken, smitten of God, and afflicted, but he was wounded for our transgressions, he was bruised for our iniquities: the chastisement of our peace was upon him; and with his stripes we are healed" (Isaiah 53:4-5 KJV). Glory to God.

"He that dwelleth in the secret place of the most High shall abide under the shadow of the Almighty. I will say of the LORD, He is my refuge and my fortress: my God; in him will I trust. Surely he shall deliver thee from the snare of the fowler, and from the noisome pestilence. He shall cover thee with his feathers, and under his wings shalt thou trust: his truth shall be thy shield and buckler. Thou shalt not be afraid for the terror by night; nor for the arrow that flieth by day; Nor for the pestilence that walketh in darkness; nor for the destruction that wasteth at noonday.A thousand shall fall at thy side, and ten thousand at thy right hand; but it shall not come nigh thee. Only with thine eyes shalt thou behold and see the reward of the wicked. Because thou hast made the LORD, which is my refuge, even the Most High, thy habitation; There shall no evil befall thee, neither shall any plague come nigh thy dwelling. For he shall give his angels charge over thee, to keep thee in all thy ways. They shall bear thee up in their hands, lest thou dash thy foot against a stone. Thou shalt tread upon the lion and adder: the young lion and the dragon shalt thou trample under feet. Because he hath set his love upon me, therefore will I deliver him: I will set him on high, because he hath known my name. He shall call upon me, and I will answer him: I will be with him in trouble; I will deliver him, and honor him. With long life will I satisfy him, and shew him my salvation." (Psalm 91 KJV)

I read three books by John Ramirez in July 2019 that helped me immensely:

- <u>Out of the Devil's Cauldron</u>, *A Journey From Darkness to Light*
- <u>Unmasking the Devil</u>, *Strategies to defeat Eternity's Greatest Enemy*
- <u>*Armed and Dangerous*</u>, *The Ultimate Battle Plan for Targeting and Defeating the Enemy*

After I read these, I realized the lady minister at that evil church had the Jezebel Spirit operating inside of her. It was text book all the things that she did and said. It matched his books like he was writing them just for me. I did not have an understanding of any of this, but after reading Ramirez' books, I am in shock as to how spot on all his descriptions are.

At this point, I think more specific information about the Jezebel Spirit, how to recognize it and what it does, will help a lot of people discern it better so it can be fought more effectively. I was not privy to this information when I was going through hell, so I hope this helps.

The Jezebel Spirit instills fear, destroys leaders and marriages, has its own agenda, and coerces and manipulates people to further its agenda, plants seeds of discord that sometimes bring divisions in the church. It gives rise to false prophets who like to practice spirit readings, witchcraft, and divination. It tries to kill off its opposition, using the spirit of murder demonic forces to take out people in the church. The Jezebel Spirit is also known for sexual abuse and causing trauma in your life. Does any of this sound familiar? Let's take a closer look next.

Chapter 8

THE JEZEBEL SPIRIT

W hat is the Jezebel Spirit? There are a variety of opinions about what constitute a Jezebel Spirit, ranging from sexual looseness in a woman to the teaching of false doctrine. The Bible does not mention a Jezebel Spirit, although it has plenty to say about Jezebel herself.

Jezebel's story is found in 1 and 2 Kings. She was the daughter of Ethbaal, the king of Tyre/Sidon and the priest of the cult of Baal, a cruel, sensuous and, revolting false god whose worship involved sexual degradation and lewdness. Ahab, king of Israel, married Jezebel and led the nation into Baal worship (1 Kings 16:31).

There are two incidents in the life of Jezebel that clearly illustrate her character and may define what is meant by the Jezebel spirit. One trait is her obsessive passion for domineering and controlling others, especially in the spiritual realm. When she became queen, Jezebel began a relentless campaign to rid Israel of all evidences of Yahweh worship. She ordered the executions of all the prophets of the Lord (1 Kings 18:4-13) and replaced their altars with those of Baal. Her strongest enemy was Elijah, who demanded a contest on Mount Carmel between the powers of Israel's God and the powers of Jezebel and the priests of Baal (1 Kings 18). Of course, God won, but despite hearing of the miraculous powers of the Lord, Jezebel refused to repent and swore on her gods that she would pursue Elijah relentlessly and take his life. Her stubborn refusal to see and submit to the power of the Living God would lead her to a hideous end (2 Kings 9:29–37).[5]

The second incident involves a righteous man named Naboth who refused to sell to Ahab a piece of land adjoining the palace, rightly declaring that to sell his inheritance would be against the Lord's command (1 Kings 21:3; Leviticus 25:23). While Ahab sulked and fumed in his bed, Jezebel taunted and ridiculed him for his weakness. Then she proceeded to have the innocent Naboth framed and stoned to death. Naboth's sons were also stoned to death to make sure there would be no heirs and the land would revert to the possession of the king. Such a single-minded determination to have one's way, no matter who is destroyed in the process, is a characteristic of the Jezebel Spirit.[5]

So infamous was Jezebel's sexual immorality and idol worship that the Lord Jesus Himself refers to her in a warning to the church at Thyatira.

> "And unto the angel of the church in Thayatira write; these things saith the Son of God, who hath his eyes like unto a flame of fire, and his feet are like fine brass; I know they works, and charity, and service, and faith, and they patience, and thy works; and the last to be more than the first. Notwithstanding I have a few things against thee, because thou sufferest that woman Jezebel, which calleth herself a prophetess, to teach and to seduce my servants to commit fornication, and to eat things sacrificed to idols. And I gave her space to repent of her fornication; and she repented not. behold, I will cast her into a bed, and them that commit adultery with her into great tribulation, except they repent of their deeds. And I will kill her children with death; and

all the churches shall know that I am he which sear-
cheth the reins and hearts: and I will give unto every
one of you according to your works. But unto you I
say, and unto the rest in Thyatira, as many as have
not this doctrine, and which have not known the
depths of Satan, as they speak; I will put upon you
none other burden. But that which ye have already
hold fast till I come. And he that over cometh, and
keepeth my works unto the end, to him will I give
power over the nations." Revelation 18-23 KJV.

Most likely referring to a woman who was influencing the early church in the same way Jezebel influenced Israel into idolatry and sexual immorality, Jesus declares to the Thyatirans that she is not to be tolerated. Whoever this woman was, like Jezebel, she refused to repent of her immorality and her false teaching. Her fate was sealed. The Lord Jesus cast her onto a sick bed, along with those who had committed idolatry with her. The end for those who succumb to a Jezebel Spirit is always death and destruction, both in the physical and the spiritual sense.

Perhaps the best way to define the Jezebel Spirit is to say it characterizes anyone who acts in the same manner as Jezebel did, engaging in immorality, idolatry, false teaching, and unrepentant sin.

Jezebel is a territorial spirit that does not inhabit a body. Ephesians 6:12 talks about spiritual forces of evil in the heavenly realm, and Jezebel is one of those along with others. Jezebel directs demons to bring damage and destruction on God's people. The Jezebel Spirit's agenda is more extensive than just control and manipulation. It is a wicked spirit that has roamed the earth for thousands of years seeking individuals to lead into sin. This spirit of seduction works people into immorality and idolatry. The plan is to steal, kill, and destroy your life.[6]

The Jezebel Spirit lets others do its dirty work. Jezebel gets another person's emotions stirred up, then lets that person go into a rage. The Jezebel Spirit sits back looking innocent, saying, "Who me? What did I do ?" The Jezebel Spirit is clever in its agenda. Having information you don't have is a powerful weapon of its control.

People under the influence of the Jezebel Spirit usually have fear issues of rejection. Generally, those cursed with the Jezebel Spirit have a history of trauma or abuse.

Those under the influence of the Jezebel Spirit often display the following behaviors. Look for them as warning signs.

- They project themselves as spiritual in an exaggerated way to gain acceptance and attention. They have their own agenda, bringing others into the fold. They play the victim and are whiney brats.
- They isolate and pit people against each other.
- They are never wrong. They blame everyone else. They play on your compassion so you won't find them out.
- They act humble, but let you know they are owed so much. They look for others who are hurt and wounded to mentor them. They operate with insecurity, and accuse others of wrong-doing to make themselves feel better.
- They initiate witchcraft-like prayers to manipulate others.

In a church environment if you are singled out by those under the Jezebel Spirit, you are in for some torment. These signs may follow you if you are targeted.

- You become fearful.
- You isolate yourself more.
- You experience unreasonable exhaustion.
- Your thoughts and dreams become sexually perverse.

- Strange and prolonged illnesses hinder you.
- Freak accidents become commonplace.[7]

Jezebel is a spirit, but it finds access through uncrucified flesh. Although the Jezebel Spirit is described in the Bible as being a woman, it does not actually have a gender. There is no doubt it functions just as proficiently through men.

We all want to believe the person with a Jezebel Spirit is delivered. The person may seem "normal" for a period, exhibiting none of the classic traits. Then suddenly, without warning, a situation will arise with the spirit once again taking control and wreaking havoc. If you recognize any Jezebel traits in your own life, begin by praying this prayer:

Father, I acknowledge I have yielded myself to the spirit of Jezebel. I come to you, humbling myself before you. I desire your standard of righteousness and holiness.

I ask you to forgive me for my tolerance of the Jezebel Spirit and for being sympathetic to its ways. Please forgive me for every way I have opened myself up to this spirit. Help me to ruthlessly reject every type of this thinking and the desire to control and manipulate other people. I renounce and bind this demon of Jezebel, and I pull down this stronghold in my life.

Through the Holy Spirit I will live by your standard of righteousness, holiness, and conduct. Open my eyes and cause Your light to expose any darkness, and help me to walk in humility and truth.[8]

Chapter 9

BREAKING GENERATIONAL CURSES

U nfortunately, some Christians mistakenly pray to Satan when they are undertaking spiritual battle. Sometimes they will address the evil one in their praying, saying something like "I bind you Satan in the name of Jesus." Be careful you are not praying to Satan. ("Father, I bind Satan in the name of Jesus.")

Instead, pray to the Father in Jesus' name. We should address our prayers to God and ask Him in the name of Jesus to bind the devil. Our prayers should always be addressed to God and God alone. See Jude 9, Mathew 12:28-29, and Revelation 20:1.[9]

"But if I cast out devils by the Spirit of God, then the kingdom of God is come unto you. Or else how can one enter into a strong man's house, and spoil his goods, except he first bind the strong man? and then he will spoil his house" (Matt. 12:28-29 KJV).

"And I saw an angel come down from heaven, having the key of the bottomless pit and a great chain in his hand" (Rev. 20:1 KJV)

Also try these suggestions: Repeat these statements out loud at regular intervals.

"I am redeemed from the curse through the blood of Jesus" (Gal. 3:13).

I break and release myself from all generational curses and iniquities as a result of my sins, and the sins of my ancestors in the name of Jesus. I break and release myself from all curses on both sides of my family back to all generations, in the name of Jesus. I break and release myself from all spoken curses and negative words spoken against me by others and by those in authority, in the name of Jesus.

It is possible to break curses that have been placed on you and/ or your family. I share what has broken the yoke of evil in my life and freed me from Satan and his evil doers.

Give your life to Jesus. The blood of Jesus removes our sin. Have faith, and trust Him.

Fight the battle with spiritual weapons. Arm yourself with the Word of God and the armor of God.

Release control over the power of your will. When Jesus shed His blood on the cross, He gave us back in return, His will, and power.

Reverse the curse and live in victory. Recognize your enemy. We do not battle flesh and blood. Our enemy is Satan, and the battle is spiritual. Forgive people who have hurt you. Treat the causes, not the symptoms, the curse is bringing to your life, such as insecurity, jealousy, and fear.

Release the power of love. Become a person whose life is transformed by love. Failing to do so allows Satan to hold you captive and keep you in bondage. Be filled with the love of God for all of His people, including yourself. Unconditional love will release God's blessing. Always forgive those who have opposed you and have sinned against you.

Develop a godly attitude. Mathew 5:45 tells how God sends rain to fall on the just and the unjust. Our attitude determines whether this rain waters you.

Align your words with His words. Your words give evidence of your faith and reflect God's Word. In other words, only speak His words and don't say anything against them. Exchange negative words for positive words. What you speak over your life determines the quality of your life. In the same manner, replace negative actions with positive actions.

Accept God's acceptance. Jesus didn't come to condemn us or punish us, but to give us hope that our lives can be different. Don't live under the burden of pain, hurt, shame, or sorrow. He does not want that for you. All the power of heaven is available to you, so set your fear aside and break every chain that binds you.

Walk in obedience. To break free of curses, be obedient to God's way. Follow the path He has planned for you. We don't have to be perfect or without mistakes, but we should do our best to move forward with God every day. Make the quality decision today to determine your own tomorrow. There is a miracle on the other side of your obedience.[10]

Chapter 10

My Healing Journey

As I have said, I come from generations of family curses, incurable sickness, lasting disease, poverty, and sexual abuse. My grandmother, my mom, and my sister have all suffered from incurable heart disease, arthritis, diabetes, and sexual abuse. The generational curses were like a death sentence to my family.

I had to stop these curses from operating in my life and my family's life. God was teaching me through studying specific places in the Word. Also, and this seems miraculous to me, but I have to mention it. I would study something in a section of the Bible and then, the same day or the next day, I would see a teaching or a sermon on the same subject on Kenneth Copland Ministries website or Believers Voice of Victory Network! They were teaching me to take responsibility and authority over sickness and disease, sexual abuse, and poverty. I did not have to be a victim to these things anymore. God was teaching me to be led by the Holy Spirit, not my emotions. I had to spend time in the word of God and let Him lead my spirit. I had to learn to take responsibility over all these bad things in my life as well as my emotional, financial, and spiritual health. I had to learn to bring all these things back into balance with what God says, back into His Wholeness.

I had to take authority over every area of my life that was out of balance. Pain was leading my life because of the abuse. If you do not take authority over the pain, then Satan will keep putting the same issues on you. So take responsibility over it with the Word of God. You need to get to the root of the problem, and the Word of God will get to the root of the problem. That is what I had to learn. Talk the Word, not the problem.

We are the only ones who have the authority to work the Word. God can't; He gave us free will for us to live by the Blessing or the Curse. I had to learn to master my life, not let it master me. I had to stop Satan from operating in my life. So if you spend time In the word of God, take authority over your life, and be led by the Holy Spirit, then you will heal. Don't let the issues in your life dictate your life.

Everything starts with believing in God, and healing our lives starts with the Word of God—not self-help books or inspirational books. These are the steps I implemented in my life to break the generational curses over me (taken from Kenneth Copland Ministries' website, kcm.org).

Believe – Believe God for the promise regarding your problem.

Speak – Speak the Word of God over the problem to turn your situation around. Everything we need starts in the spirit realm and then manifests in the physical realm.

Pray – Confess powerful scriptures, speak out loud, and pray for a break through.

Learn – Learn the Word. See what the Word says about every area of your life, every situation and problem you have. What does God's Word say about what to do for each problem area?

Apply – See how easy God's word is to apply to your situation and then change it.

So after years of abuse, I learned to follow God, keep authority over my life, and remain in obedience to God. I meditate on scripture every day. [11]

REMEMBER: BELIEVE IT, SPEAK IT,
PRAY IT, LEARN IT, TAKE IT.

Chapter 11

THE EMOTIONALLY WOUNDED SPIRIT

Do you suffer from a wounded spirit? A wounded spirit is a broken or crushed spirit. It is injury to any area of our soul and spirit faculties, our mind, emotions, and will. It is injury to the unseen part of our being.

"A man's spirit sustains him in sickness, but a crushed spirit, who can bear?" (Prov. 18:1-14).

The only way others can see the injury we suffer is through how we behave and how we conduct ourselves. Areas inside of us may be affected deeper, more in a sense of the wound. The greater the negative effect spiritually, socially, materially, and physically, the greater the wounded spirit.

Be aware of having an emotionally wounded spirit. Satan wanted to keep my soul emotionally wounded by the hurt caused by being beaten and molested as a young girl and from being violently attacked by a minister and her demons. He wanted me to stay mad at people and not forgive. He was desperate to keep me out of the will of God because now I am a huge threat to him and his plans to derail the human race. God wants us to leave our hurts behind; He wants us to master hurt. God will deliver us from hurt if we let Him.

Don't allow your past to shape your life. Don't be a victim, and, above all, don't stay mad at your past because of having made bad choices and decisions. Release your faith, but take your authority over hurt. Heaven will help you and back you up. God said we can rise above hurt emotions and feelings through the Word of God. It's impossible not to be hurt in this life, however, hurt feelings rob us of God's blessing.

> "A man shall be commended according to his wisdom: but he that is of a perverse heart shall be despised." (Prov. 12:8 KJV).

Satan has an interest in keeping you emotionally wounded by the hate you suffer. If the enemy can keep you feeling hurt, this will keep you from moving forward according to God's plan for you; you will move out of the will of God. God wants us to take authority over the spirit of hurt and bind it in heaven, hell, and earth.

"He heals the broken hearted and bandages their wounds" (Ps. 147:3 KJV).

"Wise words are like deep waters, wisdom flows from the wise like a babbling brook" (Prov. 18:4 KJV).

God's word will bring light into the darkest of souls. The enemy will keep attacking you if you keep out of the will of God. Satan will ride your emotions like a wave. He will always bring up your negative emotions so you are removed from God. Satan does not want you to get past your feelings and emotions. He will try to keep you stuck in his feeling world.

Satan will aim to keep you in drama and emotional abuse, but God will give you peace. So if you've been abused physically or emotionally, God will give back to you and heal you. If you've been violently attacked, God will heal you. Satan will take your peace away from you, but God will give back. Satan will bring sickness upon you, but God will mend you and give you back the health that was taken. This is called the grace of God.

We are called with God's anointing and the blessing. We have authority to shut down our negative emotions. Emotions are not to rule your life. When you take responsibility and authority over your feelings, then depression has no place in your life. The authority is yours to have emotional stability, and God wants us to have that authority. You are the ruler of your emotions and nobody else. Take charge over your feelings. God's work will govern your life. Don't allow emotions to take over. Master your emotional life; don't let emotions master you. It is the biggest of Satan's lies that we don't have control over our emotions. When you control your emotions, you are able to respond to situations rather than react to them.[12]

On my healing journey, I dove into the Word of God. I found and recited daily healing scriptures that addressed my emotions, and I started to understand I could take authority over all my emotions and fears. Now, I'm not perfect, but I made giant steps toward this mastery compared to where I was. Through reading and speaking healing scriptures over my emotions, God helped me heal my emotionally wounded spirit and taught me how to govern my feelings so they don't get out of control.

"Let not your heart be troubled: ye believe in God, believe also in me" (John 14:1).

"And the peace of God, which passeth all understanding, shall keep your hearts and minds through Christ Jesus" (Phil. 4:7).

"Set your affection on things above, not on things on the earth" (Col. 3:2).

"Search me, O God, and know my heart: try me, and know my thoughts" (Ps. 139:23).

Chapter 12

BE THANKFUL ALWAYS

I give thanks to God for the peace and blessings he has poured into my life. It helps me to have this list and speak it often. I suggest you do something similar to combat the effects of having a wounded spirit. It will help break that curse.

I am thankful to God, who changed my life.

I am thankful to God because I learned the truth while going through hell.

I am thankful to God because He healed me.

I am thankful to God because He loves me.

I am thankful to God for my new finances.

I am thankful to God that I have and continue to forgive and forget all the wrong and evil done to me.

I am thankful to God for my kids.

I am thankful to God for loving my family.

I am thankful to God because He showed me the way.

I am thankful to God for my wonderful boss.

I am thankful to God because He walks me in the Blessing.

I am thankful to God that He has made Satan give me back all that he has stolen from me over the years; the seven times seven what he stole back to ten generations in my family.

I am thankful to God because He has freed me and delivered me from all the snares of the fouler.

Chapter 13

HEALING AND PROTECTION SCRIPTURES THAT HAVE CHANGED MY LIFE

Understanding the basic spiritual laws of faith, also known as the fundamental laws of faith, is what Kenneth Copeland has taught for years. You have to have a grasp of these scriptures in order for any faith-based practice to manifest in your life. The cornerstone of manifestation is Faith in God to what He says. This scriptures sum it up fairly well.

> "And Jesus answering saith unto them, Therefore I say unto you, what things so ever ye desire, when ye pray, believe that ye receive *them*, and ye shall have them. And when ye stand praying, forgive, if ye have ought against any: that your Father also which is in heaven may forgive you your trespasses. But if ye do not forgive, neither will your Father which is in heaven forgive your trespasses." (Mark 11:22-26 KJV)

Surely, Jesus has borne my sickness and carried my pain. I praise God for all He has done for me. By accepting Jesus as our

Lord and Savior, we can all receive His precious salvation. His love has set me free—free from all sin, sickness, and disease. I am forever grateful for His full salvation. Now I don't have to have back pain, colds, flu, headaches, migraines or any other sickness. I am healed by His stripes. He gave me peace so nothing about me is broken, nothing about me is missing.

I spoke God's word over me many times, and I offer these scriptures that you may do the same. Whatever healing promises you need, God's Word will heal you.

"Bless the LORD, O my soul: and all that is within me, bless his holy name. Bless the LORD, O my soul, and forget not all his benefits: Who forgiveth all thine iniquities; who healeth all thy diseases; Who redeemeth thy life from destruction; who crowneth thee with lovingkindness and tender mercies; who satisfieth thy mouth with good things; so that thy youth is renewed like the eagle's." Psalm 103:1-5 KJV

> By the pardoning of sin that was taken away and kept good things from us, we are restored to God's favor. He bestows good things upon us. God is still forgiving us as we still sin and repent. He knows all of our infirmities. In his grace, he recovers his people from their decays. He fills their lives with new life and joy. (KJV commentary, Psalm 103)

"Surely he hath borne our griefs, and carried our sorrows: yet we did esteem him stricken, smitten of God, and afflicted.

But he was wounded for our transgressions, he was bruised for our iniquities: the chastisement of our peace was upon him; and with his stripes we are healed." (Isaiah 53:4-5 KJV).

These are some of the things that Jesus bought back for us on the cross: deliverance, salvation, worthiness, grace, health, new covenant (the blood), new finances, love, anointing, victory, and many more, the list is endless.

"And ye shall serve the Lord your God, and he shall bless they bread, and they water; and I will take sickness away from the midst of thee. There shall nothing cast their young, nor be barren, in thy land: the number of thy days I will fulfill" (Exodus 23:25-26 KJV).

"Who his own self bare our sins in his own body on the tree, that we, being dead to sins, should live unto righteousness; by whose stripes ye were healed" (1 Peter 2:24).

"Jesus Christ the same yesterday, today, and forever" (Hebrews 13:8).

"Christ hath redeemed us from the curse of the law, being made a curse for us: for it is written, Cursed is every one that hangeth on a tree: That the blessing of Abraham might come on the Gentiles through Jesus Christ; that we might receive the promise of the Spirit through faith" (Galatians 3:13-14 KJV).

"In fact the law requires that nearly everything be cleansed with blood and without the shedding of blood there is no forgiveness" (Hebrews 9:22).

"But if we walk in the light, we have fellowship with one another and the blood of Jesus. His son purifies us from all sin. If we claim to be without sin, we deceive ourselves and the truth is not in us, he is faithful and just and will forgive us our sins and purify us from all unrighteousness" (John 1:7-9).

"For the life of the flesh is in the blood: and I have given it to you upon the altar to make an atonement for your souls; for it is the blood that maketh an atonement for the soul" (Leviticus 17:11).

"And the blood shall be to you for a token upon the houses where ye are: and when I see the blood, I will pass over you, and the plague shall not be upon you to destroy you, when I smite the land of Egypt" (Exod. 12:13).

"In whom we have redemption through his blood, the forgiveness of sins, according to the riches of his grace" (Ephesians 1:7 KJV).

God gave us everything in the Bible to redeem us from our curses. God will restore your health when we have faith in His Word. You have authority over Satan and sickness. When Satan tries to put disease on you say, "No you don't. I have authority in Jesus' name. I do not allow sickness and disease to take command." Even if you don't see the healing right away, believe His word. Faith says to call things that are not, as though they are.

"My son, attend to my words; incline thine ear unto my sayings. Let them not depart from thine eyes; keep them in the midst of thine heart. For they are life unto those that find them, and health to all their flesh" (Proverbs 4:20-22).

Protection goes right along with healing. It did in my case, because if you're not protected you can't heal. Protection creates a safe place for us to be nurtured and brought back to center. The scriptures below are a great help to change your environment where ever you go, along with Psalm 91 and pleading the Blood.

"Just as the mountain surrounded and protected Jerusalem, so the Lord surrounds and protects his people both now and forever". (Psalms 125:2).

"But whoever listens to me will live in safety and be at ease without fear or harm". (Proverbs 1:33).

Wherever you go, by whatever means, like walking or running but particularly when traveling by car, plane, boat, train, motorcycle, plead the Blood. Even if you're going somewhere by sleigh, do so. I plead the Blood, Psalm 91, or some other protection scripture over all my travels. The Lord will keep you safe where ever you go.

I can say that I've been taught to be safe everywhere I go. I have the covenant right to be protected when I travel. Therefore, I know when I speak protection over something that Heaven dispatches whatever is needed to keep me safe, in Jesus' name. I bind Satan in heaven, hell, and earth. Everything has to go through the Blood.

"I lift up my eyes to the hills. From whence does my help come? My help comes from the Lord, who made heaven and earth. He will not let your foot be moved, he who keeps you will not slumber. Behold, he who keeps Israel will neither slumber nor sleep. The Lord is your keeper. The Lord is your shade on your right hand. The sun shall not strike you by day, nor the moon by night. The Lord shall preserve you from all evil; he will keep your life. He shall preserve your soul. The Lord shall preserve your going out and your coming in, from this time forth and even for evermore." (Psalm 121:1-8 NKJV).

A story in point. In May 2018, Mike and I finally got to take our first trip to Fort Worth, Texas to Kenneth Copeland Ministries. It was a great trip and, on our way back, I prayed protection around our plane and trip for safe passage. Soon we were approaching the Grand Rapids airport and slowing for descent. The pilot came on and said we would be landing in 15-20 minutes, and to please fasten our seat belts because it was going to be a little bumpy due to thunderstorms in the area. Well, it was more than a little bumpy. But the best part was that, just before touching down, the pilot made a strange maneuver before the runway and we touched down perfectly like laying softly on a bed.

After we landed, we got our luggage and started the hour-long drive home. When we got to Coopersville, we drove into a thunderstorm. The rain and wind got progressively worse, and we were slowed down to a crawl with very poor visibility. That's when we prayed protection around the car. We were able to keep going slowly when, all of a sudden, hail came out of the sky as big as tennis balls, beating on the car. The truck in front of us had to pull off the road because his windows got shattered. We kept going and were able to drive through the storm, but Mike was sure we would have a messed up car when we got home.

When we got the car in the garage, we checked for damage everywhere. There were no dents, there were no scratches, there wasn't even a broken headlight or taillight. Glory to God!

I love the scriptures below because this is what God will do for you. He will keep you safe no matter what.

> "Fear thou not; for I am with thee: be not dismayed; for I am thy God: I will strengthen thee; yea I will help thee; yea, I will uphold thee with the right hand of my righteousness. Behold, all they that were incensed against thee shall be ashamed and confounded: they shall be as nothing; and they that strive with thee shall perish. Thou shalt seek them, and shalt not find them, even them that contended with thee: they that war against thee shall be as nothing and as a thing of nought. For the Lord they God will hold they right hand, saying unto thee, Fear not; I will help thee. Fear not, thou worm Jacob, and ye men of Israel; I will help thee, saith the Lord, and they redeemer, the Holy One of Israel. Behold, I will make thee a new sharp threshing instrument having teeth: thou shalt thresh the mountains, and beat them small, and shalt make the hills as chaff."
> (Isaiah 41:10-15 KJV)

"As for thee also, by the blood of thy covenant I have sent forth thy prisoners out of the pit wherein is no water. Turn you to the strong hold, ye prisoners of hope: even today do I declare that I will render double unto thee." (Zechariah 9:11-12 KJV).

"Now unto him that is able to do exceeding abundantly above all that we ask or think, according to the power that worketh in us." (Ephesians 3:20 KJV).

Chapter 19

YOUR AUTHORITY IN THE NAME OF JESUS

A s I have said before, God has given you the authority to take control of your life and speak into being the desired state you want to live in. You have the right, if you're born again, to use the name of Jesus to command that authority because you are now part of God's family. You have been given power of attorney to use the name of Jesus.

In his Study Guide, *Jesus, the Name Above Every Name*, Kenneth Copeland says it I think, the best. He writes the commandment given to the Church in 1 John 3:23 is not only to love one another but to believe on the name of Jesus as well. Mark 16:17 says, "And these signs shall follow them that believe..." The name of Jesus releases the power of God to meet every person's need and set the captives free.

It is vital to see that words are important. Jesus said to speak to things—things like mountains, sycamore trees, and the sea. He told the sea "Peace be still" (Mark 4:39 KJV).

In John 17:22, Jesus prayed for us when He said, "And the glory which thou gavest me I have given them; that they may be one, even as we are one." This is the same glory and honor God displayed when He said of Jesus, "This is my beloved Son" (Matt. 3:17). He has given this to us all who believe.[13]

Jesus has given the Church His name and all the power and authority it carries. When His name is released from the mouth of a believer in faith, Satan has to flee. He recognizes the name of Jesus. He knows the power it carries.

God said, "They shall call his name Emmanuel, which being interpreted is God with us" (Matt. 1:23). The name Jesus means "Savior." This does not mean salvation alone. It means the One who gave the new birth, made man free, poured out righteousness, and injected eternal life—the God-kind of life—into the spirit of man.

Philippians 2: 9-10 says, "Wherefore God also hath highly exalted him, and given him a name which is above every name: That at the name of Jesus every knee should bow, of things in heaven, and things in earth, and things under the earth." God knew how much power and authority would have to be in the name of Jesus for it to cover the entire spectrum of Satan's existence. The name of Jesus is above every name. His name is above all sickness, poverty, worry, and any other evil work of Satan. When we use the name of Jesus, we're using the authority we have in Him.][14]

"And these signs shall follow them that believe, in my name shall they cast out devils; they shall speak with new tongues." (Mark 16:17 KJV).

"Behold, I give unto you power to tread on serpents and scorpions, and over all the power of the enemy: and nothing shall by any means hurt you." (Luke 10:19 KJV).

"Wherefore God also hath highly exalted him, and given him a name which is above every name: That at the name of Jesus every knee should bow, of things in heaven, and things in earth." (Philipians 2:9-10 KJV).

"Far above all principality, and power, and might, and dominion, and every name that is named, not only in this world, but also in that which is to come" (Ephesians 1:21 KJV).

"And his name through faith in his name hath made this man strong, whom ye see and know: yea, the faith which is by him hath given him this perfect soundness in the presence of you all." (Acts 3:16).

"And whatsoever ye do in word or deed, do all in the name of the Lord Jesus, giving thanks to God and the Father by him." (Col. 3:17).

"And whatsoever ye shall ask in my name, that will I do, that the Father may be glorified in the Son." (John 14:13).

"And Jesus came and spake unto them, saying, all power is given me in heaven and in earth. Go ye therefore, and teach all nations, baptizing them in the name of the Father, and of the Son, and of the Holy Ghost." (Matt. 28:18-19).

Once I understood my authority in Jesus' name, Satan could no longer put anything on me. Fear, arthritis, heart disease, abuse, flu, poverty, cancer, molestation—, anything attacking me could gain no foothold. Then I knew that EVERYTHING had to bow down to Him, and confess that Jesus is Lord, and nothing else. This is the biggest truth ever to be understood.

The Blood of Jesus

Pray all that you wish to see, all that you wish to declare, in the blood of Jesus. You have the authority from our heavenly Father to do so. For example, when you draw a circle around a building and you speak, "I plead the blood of Jesus Christ around this building and I draw a circle around this building. I take authority over you Satan. You cannot enter this building," then Satan cannot touch the building. So when your kids go to school, plead the blood of Jesus Christ around the building to protect them. Or when you go to work, pray protection in the blood of Jesus so Satan cannot enter that building with a gun, and he cannot touch anybody. Pray in the name of the blood of Jesus and Satan cannot touch your family or you.

Every morning I read Ephesians 16-23. I sit with the Lord and rule and reign with Him.

"I do not cease to give thanks for you, remembering you in my prayers, that the God of your Lord Jesus Christ, the father of glory, may give you a spirit of wisdom and of revelation in the knowledge of him having the eyes of your heart enlightened, that you may know what is the hope to which he has called you. And you he made alive when you were dead through the trespasses and sins in which you once walked, following the course of this world, following the prince of the power of the air the spirit that is new at work in the sons of disobedience. Among these we all once lived in the passions of our flesh Following the desire of body and mind, and so we were by natural children of wrath, like the rest of mankind. But God who is rich in mercy, out of the great love with which he loved us, even when we were dead through our trespasses, made us live together with Christ by grace you have been saved, and raised us up with him in the heavenly places in Christ Jesus. For by grace you have been saved through faith.

What are the riches of his glorious inheritance in the saints? And what is the immeasurable greatness of his power in us who believe, according to the working of his great might which he accomplished in Christ when he raised him from the dead made him sit at the right hand in the heavenly places." (Ephesians 1:16-23).

I pray over family, friends, financial matters, and whatever else God places before me as well as whatever assignment He wants me to do. This I do daily.

"No weapon that is formed against me shall prosper. Any tongue that shall rise against you in judgement you shall show to be in the wrong" (Isa. 54:17).

Chapter 15

UNDERSTANDING THE ANOINTING

The Anointing makes the whole body fit together perfectly, as each part does its own special work. It helps other parts grow so the whole body is healthy growing and full of love (Eph. 4:16 KJV). The Anointing is designed to destroy all burdens and yokes, and to put everything back together like nothing ever happened. Satan does not want people to know about The Anointing.

> "And it shall come to pass in that day, that his burden shall be taken away from off thy shoulder, and his yoke from off thy neck, and the yoke shall be destroyed because of the anointing" (Isa. 10:27 KJV).

I will never forget when I started studying on my own, watching sermons from Bill Winston Ministries (BWM) and Kenneth Copland Ministries (KCM), about The Anointing. The Anointing is designed to reverse the Curse (the original curse after the fall, as well as any others you come across during your life) and put you back together like nothing ever happened, plus give you power from the Holy Spirit. It makes all the parts of the body, mind, spirit, and soul work in harmony together to accomplish whatever the assignment is from God.

From experience, I immediately knew Satan does not want anyone to know about this. When I spoke Isaiah 10:27, I heard Satan say "You just destroyed everything I've been building!" I was so excited to break his stronghold I spoke that scripture all the rest of the day. It was enjoyable to say the least. It electrified me with power, and I enjoyed listening to Satan scream in pain all the rest of the day.

"The Spirit of the Lord is upon me, because he hath anointed me to preach the gospel to the poor; he hath sent me to heal the brokenhearted, to preach deliverance to the captives, and recovering of sight to the blind, to set at liberty them that are bruised" (Luke 4:18 KJV).

"But the anointing which ye have received of him abideth in you, and ye need not that any man teach you: but as the same anointing teacheth you of all things, and is truth, and is no lie, and even as it hath taught you, ye shall abide in him" (1 John 2:27 KJV).

The first thing we have to recognize is God anoints His people for a purpose. Next, notice that the scriptures don't say how God anointed the Son of God with the Holy Ghost.

"Then God anointed Jesus of Nazareth with the Holy Ghost and with power. He went about doing good and healing all that were oppressed of the devil, for God was with him" (Acts 10:38 KJV).

Whatever Satan has done wrong to you in your life, plus whatever you have done to screw your life up, God will put it back together just like it never happened. That's His promise to you and me. God will put His anointing on you so you may get your assignment done for Him in short order.

Chapter 16

FOR GOD IS A GOD OF JUSTICE: RECOMPENSE AND VENGEANCE

I want you to read this passage from Psalm 94. Vengeance takes all the fear out of your assignment, everything. There is an anointing on vengeance. Anything that Satan does wrong to you, to me, to anyone who is God's property, God will judge. Any corner you turn, and anything done wrong to you, God will make him pay damages and restoration, nothing will escape him. So when I understood what vengeance meant for me, It made me bolder than a lion. Yes, God will actually fight for your peace.

> "O Lord God, to whom vengeance belongeth; O God, to whom vengeance belongeth, shew thyself. Lift up thyself, thou judge of the earth: render a reward to the proud. LORD, how long shall the wicked, how long shall the wicked triumph? How long shall they utter and speak hard things? and all the workers of iniquity boast themselves? They break in pieces thy people, O LORD, and afflict thine heritage. They slay the widow and the stranger, and murder the fatherless. Yet they say, The LORD shall not see, neither shall the God of Jacob regard it. Understand, ye brutish among the people: and ye

fools, when will ye be wise? He that planted the ear, shall he not hear? he that formed the eye, shall he not see? He that chastiseth the heathen, shall not he correct? He that teacheth man knowledge, shall not he know? The LORD knoweth the thoughts of man, that they are vanity. Blessed is the man whom thou chastenest, O LORD, and teachest him out of thy law; That thou mayest give him rest from the days of adversity, until the pit be digged for the wicked. For the LORD will not cast off his people, neither will he forsake his inheritance. But judgment shall return unto righteousness: and all the upright in heart shall follow it. Who will rise up for me against the evildoers? or who will stand up for me against the workers of iniquity? Unless the LORD had been my help, my soul had almost dwelt in silence. When I said, My foot slippeth; thy mercy, O LORD, held me up. In the multitude of my thoughts within me thy comforts delight my soul. Shall the throne of iniquity have fellowship with thee, which frameth mischief by a law? They gather themselves together against the soul of the righteous, and condemn the innocent blood. But the LORD is my defense; and my God is the rock of my refuge. And he shall bring upon them their own iniquity, and shall cut them off in their own wickedness; yea, the LORD our God shall cut them off. (Psalm 94 1-15 KJV).

"For we know him that hath said, Vengeance belongeth unto me, I will recompense, saith the Lord. And again, The Lord shall judge his people." (Heb. 10:30 KJV).

I was given an assignment to take care of a friend in Florida. I noticed that anyone who came against me with drama, or gave my friend or me a hard time over anything, God removed them very quickly so those people could not cause a disruption. It was strange how He would remove them out and we would never hear from them again.

"He said, 'Look up and see, all the rams which are mating [with the flock] are streaked, speckled, and spotted; for I have seen all that Laban has been doing to you." (Gen. 31:12 AMP)

I know God has seen everything the demonic forces have done to me, and He will make them pay damages. If you have been molested, violently attacked, traumatized, beaten, or even left for dead, God will make recompense for you and nobody will ever mistreat you again. God has seen it and He knows what your abuser has done.

"If I whet my glittering sword, and mine had take hold on judgment; I will render vengeance to mine enemies, and will reward them that hate me" (Deut. 32:41 KJV).

> "If it be possible, as much as lieth in you, live peaceably with all men. Dearly beloved, avenge not yourselves, but rather give place unto wrath: for it is written, Vengeance is mine; I will repay, saith the Lord. Therefore if thine enemy hunger, feed him; if he thirst, give him drink: for in so doing thou shalt heap coals of fire on his head. Be not overcome of evil, but overcome evil with good."(Rom. 12: 17-21 KJV)

The line of our duty is clearly marked out, and if our enemies are not melted by persevering kindness, we are not to seek vengeance; they will be consumed by the fiery wrath of that God to whom vengeance belongs. The last verse suggests what is not easily understood by the world; that in all strife and contention, those that revenge are conquered, and those that forgive are conquerors. Be not overcome of evil. Learn to defeat ill designs against you.[17]

Chapter 17

CHOOSE FORGIVENESS

F orgiving people is easy; it's a choice. Repenting is easy; it is also a choice. I'd rather forgive and repent than drink poison. We don't have to like what others have done to us, however, the more you forgive the hurtful person, the easier it gets. It is best to ask God to bless that person and that releases you, which in turn allows God to work on that person to change them for the better. Satan puts challenging people in your path to test your ability to forgive.

I follow these four steps in seeking to forgive those who have wronged me.

1. Choose to forgive.
2. Release those who hurt you by forgiving them.
3. Bless those who hurt you.
4. Believe God is healing your emotions.

Concerning that horrible lady minister, the more I said "I forgive you" and the more I prayed for her, the more I realized God was healing my insides.[15] The more I gave forgiveness, the harder it was to believe that this woman was trying to kill me. I was releasing her. I was being healed.

There is an anointing on forgiveness that will set you free and break that yoke.[16]

See what the scripture instructs about forgiveness.

"Bless them that persecute you: bless and curse not." (Rom. 12:14).

"Bless them that curse you, and pray for them which spitefully use you." (Luke 6:28).

"But I say unto you, Love your enemies, bless them that curse you, do good to them that hate you, and pray for them which despitefully use you, and persecute you." (Matt. 5:44).

"And the Lord turned the captivity of Job, when he prayed for his friends: also the Lord gave Job twice as much as he had before." (Job 42: 10).

Pray for your enemies. Ask God to bring them into the realization they can't harm you. Pray that these people do not remain deceived. Pray for people who ridicule you and proclaim falsehoods over you. Pray for those who abuse you and violently attack you. Ask God to remove the evil coming at you and to help you love those who persecute you.

We find courage in forgiveness. Things we never know to expect come from forgiving one another without any expectations.

"There is no fear in love, but perfect love drives out fear because fear to do is punishment. The one who fears is not made perfect in love" (1 John 4:18).

"We know how much God loves us, and we have put our trust in his love. God is love and all who live in love live in God and God's love is in them" (1 John 4:16).

Unconditional love is very powerful. When we love unconditionally, and when we receive unconditional love, we find there is power in those feelings, and it activates us.

Chapter 18

HEALING COMES FULL CIRCLE

"**B**ut if he be found, he shall restore sevenfold; he shall give all the substance of his house" (Prov. 6:31).

"For it is the day of the Lord's vengeance, and the year of recompenses for the controversy of Zion" (Isa. 34:8).

After years of being away, my sister told me that my mom was sick. I knew God wanted her to see me so we got together at my sister's place. It was good. My kids loved seeing her. There were lots of hugs. I showed her pictures of the kids growing up. She loved seeing my kids. Tony was three and a half, and Laura was seven at the time. My daughter called her Gramma right away. I noticed sometime during the visit that I did not feel any more pain in my body. My heart was healed, and forgiveness had taken place.

I asked God if my mom had ever loved me, and He had me call her on the phone and ask her. When I did, she said, "Yes, I really love you. I'm sorry. I really had a hard life, but I love you all." Upon hearing that, I had a heart full of love and compassion for her. I was instantly healed and loved her back.

I was really surprised by my daughter and my son. They were so small, but immediately loved her. I was astonished by how well the kids took to her and that I could heal so fast, literally in an instant. I never really meant to stay away for as long as I did. We had more visits from then on and they were better each time.

God gave Mom and me about a year together before she died. Because of my experiences with my mother, I never tell people to walk away, but rather to please forgive. Remember, Satan is behind destroying your family.

After Mom died, I helped my step-dad the last six months of his life while he battled cancer. I bought all his food, cleaned his house, and did a lot to help him out when he had nothing. I told him it was time to heal, he and his kids, and he did say in the end that he was sorry for all the stuff that happened. He thanked me for helping him so much; it was God's grace.

My parents and I all healed in the end and forgave each other, but we never talked about the abuse. I let it all go, all the terrible things that happened. I forgave the other men who hurt me too. Those men never said they were sorry, but I forgave them. I forgave them all with His help.

As for the lady minister, she never said she was sorry. She only said I deserve it. I did some deep inner healing with God over this, employing the scriptures, and He helped heal me on the inside.

God is awesome; listen to Him. He knows what we need. He will heal you. Recompense and vengeance is His and His alone. You do not and should not take that upon you. Let God go after your enemies. Forgive them, and He will give you double for your trouble—seven times seven back to you!

I love God. He really did help me. He saved me, helped me to build a bridge to Him and others, and pulled the walls down so I could become whole. Please make the same choice. I'm glad I did.

"For your shame ye shall have double; and for confusion they shall rejoice in their portion: therefore in their land they shall possess the double: everlasting joy shall be unto them. For I the Lord love judgment, I hate robbery for burnt offering; and I will direct their work in truth, and I will make an everlasting covenant with them" (Isaiah 61:7-8).

Chapter 19

THE BLESSING AND WHAT IT HAS DONE FOR ME

The Blessing is best spelled out in Deuteronomy 28. I include the passage here for you to take to heart.

"And it shall come to pass, if thou shalt hearken diligently unto the voice of the Lord thy God, to observe and to do all his commandments which I command thee this day, that the LORD thy God will set thee on high above all nations of the earth.

And all these blessings shall come on thee, and overtake thee, if thou shalt hearken unto the voice of the Lord thy God.

Blessed shalt thou be in the city, and blessed shalt thou be in the field.

Blessed shall be the fruit of thy body, and the fruit of thy ground, and the fruit of thy cattle, the increase of thy kine, and the flocks of thy sheep.

Blessed shall be thy basket and thy store.

Blessed shalt thou be when thou comest in, and blessed shalt thou be when thou goest out.

The Lord shall cause thine enemies that rise up against thee to be smitten before thy face: they shall come out against thee one way, and flee before thee seven ways.

The Lord shall command the blessing upon thee in thy storehouses, and in all that thou settest thine hand unto; and he shall bless thee in the land which the LORD thy God giveth thee.

The Lord shall establish thee a holy people unto himself, as he hath sworn unto thee, if thou shalt keep the commandments of the LORD thy God, and walk in his ways.

And all people of the earth shall see that thou art called by the name of the Lord; and they shall be afraid of thee.

And the Lord shall make thee plenteous in goods, in the fruit of thy body, and in the fruit of thy cattle, and in the fruit of thy ground, in the land which the Lord swore unto thy fathers to give thee.

The Lord shall open unto thee his good treasure, the heaven to give the rain unto thy land in his season, and to bless all the work of thine hand: and thou shalt lend unto many nations, and thou shalt not borrow.

And the Lord shall make thee the head, and not the tail; and thou shalt be above only, and thou shalt not be beneath; if that thou hearken unto the commandments of the Lord thy God, which I command thee this day, to observe and to do them." (Deuteronomy 28:1-13 KJV)

The Blessing is awesome. Be obedient to God and do what He says, and The Blessing will go to work for you. It knows what to do.

After years of abuse and vicious attacks from demonic forces, God one day showed me 2 Timothy 1:7: "For he didn't give me a spirit of fear, he gave me love, power, and a sound mind." That verse healed me. There was no more fear inside me, just like that. I finally learned I did not need to be afraid all the time of what the enemy could do to me. Satan no longer had any power over me. The anointing had broken the yoke of the curse, and I was free. I still am.

And then, I said every day, several times a day, "By his stripes I'm healed, and I take authority over it." I was filled with peace, God's peace! The vile attacks stopped. I was healed in Jesus' name. Yes, Satan would try to come back and pester me, but he knows I know he is finished and does not have any power over me at all. All his words are empty. I know the truth. I was healed 2,000 years ago through Jesus Christ, and Satan can no longer work his evil on me.

I want you to know I had to become a doer of the word of God, not just a reader. I had to say God's word out loud and believe it. You can't just read or speak it once and stop there. You need to act on it often, even every day, and Satan will flee like a leaf in the wind. I became the righteousness in Him.

God could not do for me until I realized my authority; that He has given it to me to do for myself in His name. I learned everything has a name and has to bow to Him. Nothing is above Him and all have to confess that Jesus is Lord!

> "Wherefore God also hath highly exalted him, and
> given him a name which is above every name:
> That at the name of Jesus every knee should bow,
> of things in heaven, and things in earth, and things
> under the earth; And that every tongue should

confess that Jesus Christ is Lord, to the glory of
God the Father." (Phil. 2:9-11).

Fear and disease have many names: cancer and arthritis, poverty and sickness. All manner of evil has a name, and, let me tell
you, all names must bow down to Him. *All names*.

God didn't put on me any sickness and any curse; those all
come from Satan. If it steals, kills, or destroys, it's always from him.

Chapter 20

My Stories of Faith and God's Blessings

I want to share my testimony of how God worked two wonderful and amazing blessings in my family's life. I can only point out through these stories how God protects those who love Him and follow His word from the evil workings of Satan.

In 2015, my son, who was I think twenty at the time, bought himself a shiny, new Red Mazda 3. He was proud of his car and the great deal he got on it. We knew he loved that car just by the way he acted when he left home with it. He wagged and zoomed with that car every time.

For some time at this point, my husband and I had been pleading the blood of Jesus over our family and speaking Psalm 91, especially for our kids as they needed all the help they could get. I believe this made a huge difference in what happened next.

One Sunday evening, our son was driving to a friend's house down Old Grand Haven Road. It was fairly late, though it was a clear, calm October night. My son really wasn't paying attention to anything in particular as he drove along, but he did notice a spark along the roadway far ahead. He did not think anything of it.

Next he noticed a dark vehicle way far up the way, but he was not able to make out the make or how it was positioned on the side of the road. Driving the speed limit with nobody around, he got up to the spot where the vehicle had been but it was gone. All of a sudden, his car careened to the other side of the road and he blacked out.

When he woke up, his car was shoved over onto the side of the road. He called 911 and gave them his location. Then he called his dad and a girlfriend to come help him. He couldn't start the car and got upset, so he got out and walked around the car. It was wrecked, and there was a huge electrical line caught up under his front axle and around his tires.

He grabbed the line from under his tires and proceeded to yank with all his might to get his car untied from the electrical line. He could not budge it. Just then the police and fire department pulled up telling him to let go of the line because it was still live! (An ambulance arrived also but my son declined medical treatment.)

We think when he caught the wire, it grabbed his car and threw it to the other side of the road. He had his seat belt on, so, as his car swung around, he must have bumped his head on the driver's side window because it was shattered. If you know my son, he has a very hard head so it did not hurt him a bit. Everybody moved away from the car, and the fire department got the line shut off by the power company.

My son's car was totaled and the electronics were fried because of contact with the power line. So why was my son untouched? Why was the car fried and not my son? We are convinced the blood of Jesus and the fact we were speaking the Word, namely Psalm 91, over him daily protected him from harm.

My next story occurred a few months later. Mike and I were out of money, out of time, and out of options. It was summer and our car was failing. It was an old 2002 Escort hatchback my husband and I were sharing.

Michael was working his hiney off at Home Depot. I was merchandising c.d.'s and videos at a Meijer store, working no more than fifteen hours a week. I had been trying for a long time to upgrade and change jobs, but the devil was keeping me trapped in isolation. We just could not cut a break. Everything was breaking down. My husband was fixing things literally every other day.

So I filled myself up with the Word with resources from Kenneth Copland Ministries, aka Eagle Mountain International Church, and Jesse Duplantis Ministries. I used both their websites and ordered as many products as I could to learn the Word as fast as I could. Mike and I were believing for a car, more income, some favor, anything to boost us up a little. We were sowing seed by putting money into a ministry and asking God for the hundred fold return (this is part of The Blessing). We listened to Jesse Duplantis a lot and began believing and sowing.

We discovered Jesse had a speaking engagement planned for Bishop Keith Butler's church in Southfield, MI. That was only three hours away. We wondered how would we get there because we could not use the Escort on the highway for such a long trip. My son was using a rental car because of his accident. so we borrowed the little Hyundai and took off early Sunday morning for Southfield.

When we got to the event, we were blown away. Jesse spoke the full day and it was phenomenal. We really had our faith renewed. We sowed our last fifty dollars into JDM's ministry and asked God for a car. We didn't even have money to get a meal after that. Instead, we just drove home. We didn't even have enough money to put more gas in the tank on the way back.

Reaching Muskegon around 4pm, with the tank on fumes, we safely made it home. We parked our son's car and were lucky enough to be invited over to my husband's parents' house for a family dinner. We said yes because we were starving. We hopped in the Escort to go visiting and were treated to a steak dinner! Not only that, but during the course of dinner, Gramma and Grampa had something to tell us. They said they knew we were having a tough time of it and they wanted to get us a new car—right out of the blue, with no information from us as we had not said anything to anyone. That's how we knew this gift, this blessing was from God.

Michael's parents told us to find a car we liked and then let them know when we were ready to buy it. We found a nice Malibu at Shoreline Motors with leather seats, loaded, and with great A/C and heat. They wrote us a check for $10,000.

That's how we got a new car from God—from a $50.00 seed sowed in the right place. Only four hours elapsed from the time we asked God for His assistance, to the time we learned we were going to get a remarkable gift from Gramma and Grandpa. Glory to God!

This is the end of the book, but it is not the end of the story. Above were only a few examples of the enormous amount of blessings that we have walked through since our journey began. The rest of them I'd really like to talk about in another book, because its going to take another book just to sum up the mind boggling, awesome things that God has showered upon us. I can't wait to see what happens next.

SALVATION PRAYER

I f you died today do you know where you would go, for eternity? Like forever with no time. If your not sure, and you've never made Jesus the Lord of your life. I encourage you to invite him into your heart now. Your life will never be the same. I'm not talking about religion, I'm talking about a relationship. If you would, just pray this simple prayer below and mean it with all of your heart.

Heavenly Father, I come to you in the name of Jesus. Your word says whoever shall call on the name of the Lord shall be saved (Acts 2:21).

I am calling on you. I pray and ask Jesus to come into my heart and be the Lord of my life. According to Romans 10:9-10, "If thou shall confess with thy mouth that Jesus is Lord, and shall believe in thine heart that God has raised him from the dead, then thou shall be saved. For with the heart men believeth unto righteousness, and with the mouth confession is made unto salvation."

Father, I do that now. I confess Jesus is Lord and I believe in my heart You raised Him from the dead. I repent of sin; I renounce it. I renounce the devil and everything he stands for. Jesus is my Lord. In Jesus' name, Amen.

If you prayed that prayer. Tell someone.

BIBLIOGRAPHY AND FOOTNOTES

Ramirez, John. "Out of the Devil's Cauldron, A Jouney From Darkness to Light", © 2012 Heaven and Earth Media a division of John Ramirez Ministries, Pgs. 82-114

3, 4

Ramirez, John. "Unmasking the Devil, Strategies to Defeat Eternity's Greatest Enemy, © 2015 Destiny Image Publishers Inc. Pgs. 145-161

1

Ramirez, John. "Armed and Dangerous The Ultimate Battle Plan for Targeting and Defeating the Enemy." © 2017 Chosen Books a Division of Baker Books. Pgs. 72-81

Bradley, Michael. "What is the Jezebel Spirit and How it Operates." www.bible-knowledge.com/the-jezebel spirit. © 2005 – 2019, Thomas Nelson, Inc.

5, 7, 8, 10

Copeland, Kenneth. "Healing Getting Started." www.kcm.org. © 1997-2019 Eagle Mountain International Church Inc. aka Kenneth Copeland Ministries.

11
Copeland, Kenneth. "Jesus, the Name Above Every Name Study Guide", © 1983, Kenneth Copeland Publications. Eagle Mountain International Church, pgs. 17-44

13,14

Houdman, S. Michael. "What is the Jezebel Spirit." www.gotquestions.org.© 2002-2019, Got Questions Ministries.

2, 6, 9, 10

Hutch, Larry, "9 Ways to Break a Generational Curse." www.charismamag.com. © 2014

8,9,10

Ibbitson, Don. "12 Warning Signs a Person Is Under the Influence of the Jezebel Spirit", www.aandbcounseling.com. © 2018, Above and Beyond Counseling.

Meyer, Joyce. Beauty for Ashes: Receiving Emotional Healing, © 1994, Harrison House Publishing, pg. 118

15.

Dollar, Creflo. "2019 Taking Authority Over Emotions", March 25,26,27 2019., You Tube Video and Sermons., World Changers Church International.

12,

Dollar, Creflo. "2019 Taking Authority Over Hurt Feelings", April 2019, You Tube Video and Sermons, World Changers Church International

16

Winston, Bill. "Vengeance of the Lord Sermon Series", April 30 and May 1, 2019, You Tube Video Series, Bill Winston Ministries Inc.

17

ABOUT THE AUTHOR

K athy Jennings lives with her husband of over thirty-three years. They have two grown children. She spends her time on assignment for God, working to help others from all over to recover from an abusive past.

Kathy is a K.C.M. partner and is an E-member of Eagle Mountain International Church.